RECOGNITION, GRATITUDE & CELEBRATION

RECOGNITION, GRATITUDE & CELBRATION

PATRICK L. TOWNSEND
JOAN GEBHARDT

CRISP PUBLICATIONS

Editor-in-Chief: *William F. Christopher*

Managing Editor: *Kathleen Barcos*

Editor: *Amy Marks*

Cover Design: *Kathleen Barcos*

Cover Production: *Russell Leong Design*

Book Design & Production: *London Road Design*

Printer: *Bawden Printing*

Library of Congress Card Catalog Number 97-66243

ISBN 1-56052-432-4

For
Ruth Gebhardt
and
Katherine Townsend

CONTENTS

I.

Polite Is Also Politic

Y OU ARE NINE YEARS OLD. It is the day after your
birthday and you are seated at the kitchen table
with a stack of stationery in front of you, chewing
on the end of a pen. You have been given a task to
accomplish before you can go out and play. What is it?
You guessed it: You have to finish those pesky thank
you notes.

It wouldn't be such a chore if people always gave you
something you really wanted. But they don't. Aunt Hazel
sent paisley pajamas that you swore silently you'd never
wear, and what could have possessed Uncle Milton to
select a book of poetry? And yet, and yet . . . You still feel
a glow that they both remembered you. Aunt Hazel is a
nice lady, and you know she deserves recognition for her
effort. Then, too, Uncle Milton sent a baseball glove last
year, and he even plays catch when he comes over for
dinner. Maybe he didn't hit the bull's-eye this time, but
you do want him to keep trying, don't you?

There in a nutshell are the two reasons for saying
thank you: one emotional and one rational. People

deserve a thank you not only when they make a special effort, but when you want them to repeat the effort, too. At nine years old you may have needed help figuring out that saying thank you strengthens relationships and encourages desired behavior. Adults, however, know that when it comes to saying thank you, good manners and good sense are the same. They know that saying thank you is not only polite, but also politic. Or do they?

II.

Saying Thank You
Is Good Business

"IT'S NOT MY JOB to say thank you." The speaker
was the president of a Baby Bell company; the
setting was a workshop taught by a team of
consultants for the top thirty senior managers. A silence
descended. One consultant observed quietly that he didn't
consider saying thank you a job, he found it a pleasure
to speak to people about their accomplishments. There
was no response. The other, less-tactful consultant asked
if anyone in the room would enjoy hearing thank you
from the president. The response was eloquent. People
began dropping pencils, checking the contents of pockets,
fiddling with papers–anything to avoid catching the
president's eye.

Everyone likes to hear thank you. Why then is
it so hard to say? Some of it may be left over from the
time when you were nine years old and people didn't do
exactly what you expected or you just couldn't find the
words. In a business environment, however, the failure
to say thank you more often than not signals a misguided

Figure 1. Saying thank you is good business

attempt to maintain a purely rational relationship between people.

When Reason Becomes Unreasonable

How often have you heard, "I don't have to say thank you for that—that's their job"? It sounds sane enough, but it's really a mini temper tantrum. Think of it this way: There are written job descriptions and de facto job descriptions. What counts is what happens on a day-to-day, week-to-week basis. Whatever someone did in the period before the last paycheck is—by agreement—the de facto job description. When someone goes beyond that and does something that you want done on a regular basis, the only truly rational thing to do is to mark the occasion by saying thank you. Only by doing so can you hope to have that new behavior become part of what happens as a matter of course. Saying thank you goes a long way toward locking in an improvement by giving it official sanction. The alternative is to get on your high horse and run roughshod over any improvement.

The Downside of the Rational Approach

Not everyone, of course, displays such a narrow-minded approach. There are even elegant attempts to keep relationships purely rational: These are commonly known as incentive programs. In incentive programs, the employee is offered a quid pro quo for predefined accomplishments, usually in the form of a percentage of savings or a bonus or something of substantial monetary value. When the incentive is linked to cash, the manager can avoid the need for an emotional involvement—or personal contact of any sort—by delivering the incentive in the employee's pay envelope. When the incentive is linked to merchandise, the emotional component is usually stronger but not necessarily personal. There still may be no interaction between the giver and the recipient. Best of all, incentives appear to be so fair: Someone does something special, they get something special. Yet a negative emotional overlay remains. The word "bribe" comes to mind. So do the words "winner" and "loser." All are a far cry from "thank you."

Thank you taps into a different set of emotional responses. It implies recognition, gratitude and celebration. Thank you is profoundly personal. Although incentive and bonus programs are certainly workable and have a long history of leading to positive results, they don't replace a program to say thank you; at best, they can supplement such a program. Nor do regular promotions and salary increases act as replacements. Both of them are designed to meet fair payment standards. The extra effort, the identification with the good of the organization, the joy of a job well done—the intangibles—get short shrift if salary payments and job promotions are all that happen.

The most absurd argument against saying thank you with some kind of gift or ceremony is mounted by purists who insist, "If we start rewarding improvements, employees will start looking for ways to improve for the wrong reason." Does anyone really care about anyone else's private motivation as long as their behavior contributes to the organization's improvement? The question is, rather, Does the company want the employees to continue behaving in this new, improved way? And what is so wrong about the very human need for encouragement and praise?

Linking Leadership and Thank You

Saying thank you not only inspires recipients, it also leads to personal growth on the part of the person astute enough to employ those words. Recognizing the achievements of others, expressing gratitude and celebrating successes are all acts—and responsibilities—of leadership. Two

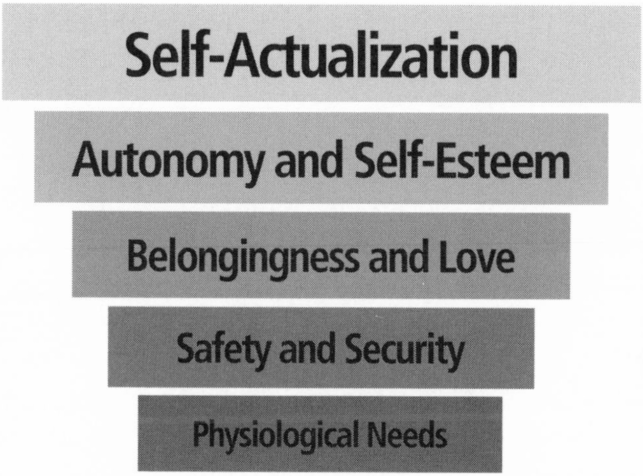

Self-Actualization

Autonomy and Self-Esteem

Belongingness and Love

Safety and Security

Physiological Needs

Figure 2.   Maslow's hierarchy of needs

definitions of leadership apply here: one that defines leadership relative to its cousin concept, management, and one that simply defines leadership.

Quite simply, a manager cares that a job gets done, whereas a leader cares not only that the job gets done—he or she also cares about the people who do the job. In short, a leader cares about other people. Leaders not only care, they take action—which leads to the second definition of leadership:

> *Leadership is the creation of an*
> *environment in which others can self-actualize*
> *in the process of completing the job.*

7

Leaders not only see others as individuals and value their contributions, they also work to create circumstances that enable followers to meet basic needs for self-esteem and growth. When you acknowledge how well someone does their job, when you provide the information and tools they need to perform to the peak of their abilities, when you make sure they know that you appreciate their job performance and how it fits into the overall scheme of things, you are helping that person move to the top of behavioral theorist Abraham Maslow's Hierarchy of Needs (see Figure 2).

John Ball, Service Training Manager at American Honda Motor Company, makes this connection between saying thank you, leadership and action:

> *I try to remember that people—good, intelligent, capable people—may actually need day-to-day thanks for the job they do. I try to remember to get up out of my chair, turn off my computer, go sit or stand next to them and see what they're doing, ask about the challenges, find out if they need additional help, offer that help if possible, and most of all, tell them in all honesty that what they are doing is important: to me, to the company and to our customers.[1]*

Management is a subset of leadership, a subset without that something extra. Managers, for instance, often allow the "no news is good news" approach to determine their habits for contacting people. They operate on the basis of, "If they don't hear from me, employees should assume that all is well; and if I don't hear from them, I should be able to assume that all is well." Leaders take every opportunity to make contact, and when no opportunity exists naturally, they make the opportunity. The result is a strong emotional bond based on mutual trust.

Training to Say Thank You

Fortunately, as with every other aspect of being a leader, training and growth can take place in the area of saying thank you. The starting point may be as simple as talking about it. In an ideal world the senior person in the organization would lead the discussion of why and how to say thank you. In a not-quite-ideal world, anyone (including an outside person, possibly even a paid consultant) could lead the discussion. Such a dialogue can be the first step in helping an executive let go of old ideas about incentives and a purely rational workplace. The trick will be to get everyone to take part. Silence does not necessarily mean consent. It could mean that the nonparticipant has decided to ignore any group conclusions. Individual study, perhaps in the form of assigned reading, is also appropriate.

Saying Thank You Isn't Always Easy

What cannot happen is for an organization's senior management to assume that this aspect of being a leader is natural for everyone. Saying thank you—especially taking part in the emotional aspects of expressing gratitude—does not come easily to everyone. For some people it means a radical change in behavior. This is not entirely un-expected. Some parents, for instance, are much better at giving their children practical toys (or checks) than they are at giving them hugs of either the physical or mental variety.

But the Benefits Are Worth It

There are benefits for individuals who overcome their personal inhibitions about saying thank you (see Figure 3). For example, saying thank you is fun—once the basics are mastered. It provides an oasis in a pressure-packed day, something to look forward to for both the manager and the person(s) being thanked. It may come as a surprise, but feeling good at work—feeling good about your individual contribution or about other people's reaction when you take note of their contributions—is neither illegal nor immoral.

Then, too, a manager who regularly says thank you will find himself or herself with a reputation for being a good leader. Leadership is in the eye of the follower, and there is no better way to ensure that others form a positive opinion of you. Everyone likes to hear someone say thank you, and it is only human nature to think well of anyone who makes the effort.

An unexpected dividend of saying thank you is that managers become recipients of information to which they might otherwise not be privy. People are eager to tell someone what they have done and what they are working on, especially if they expect to receive praise for it. Those exchanges can be invaluable when it comes time for a manager to make decisions about promotions, pay raises, budget allocations, restructuring, or selection of a special team for a high-visibility project. The manager will have faces to go with names and will know individual strengths and the combinations of coworkers that have clicked in the past. In short, managers who say thank you will be able to do a far better job of managing their piece of the organization as well as their own future.

Blending the Rational and Emotional

Saying thank you, as with almost everything that happens in the name of leadership or quality or any other worthwhile effort in the workplace, is a blend of things rational and things emotional. On the personal level, the emotional component is the fun; the rational component is the personal growth. On the organizational level, the emotional component is the warm glow that comes with being thanked. Someone on an assembly line or in an executive suite deserves to feel that sensation as much as a kind rela-

---

- **Enjoyment of your time on this planet**

- **Growth toward being a leader**

- **Rewarding reputation with seniors and subordinates**

- **Positive connection with your subordinates**

- **Knowledge of the capabilities of your subordinates**

Figure 3.   Personal benefits of saying thank you

tive does. The rational component is that organizations continue to benefit from efforts to improve. And one of the ways to ensure continual improvement is by saying thank you.

Improving employee behavior.   Saying thank you has a positive, long-lasting effect on employee behavior. If people enjoy their jobs, if going to work is not a life sentence to hard labor, they are going to do a better job. When employees are allowed, encouraged or otherwise helped to take pride in their accomplishments, to appreciate the inevitable humor in their surroundings, and to have an honest appreciation for the relative importance of their various tasks, they are able to work more efficiently and more effectively.

Increasing employee satisfaction.   Saying thank you is part of keeping employees satisfied with the company. In virtually every "why I stay with my current company" survey, financial compensation (even at very high levels) ranks significantly behind feeling appreciated. According to "Rethinking Rewards," an article in the Harvard Business Review, the primary motivations for employees are (in decreasing significance): (a) a sense of accomplishment in performing the work itself, (b) recognition from peers and top management, (c) career advancement, (d) management support, and, only then, (e) salary.[2]

A metaphor for this finding can be drawn from family life: How many divorces have been initiated because "he/she never pays attention to me" when the offending partner thought that bringing home the paycheck and "being there" was all that was needed? If nothing else, an effort to say thank you is certain to reduce a company's employee turnover rate, with all its direct costs (e.g., the expenditures for recruitment and catch-up training) and indirect costs (e.g., the loss of experience and knowledge that the departing employee takes with her or him).

Other benefits. Saying thank you, however, does much more. It supports successful quality efforts by encouraging employees to look for opportunities to make improvements. Even little improvements add up. The Quality Revolution suggests that, over time, incremental improvements are as powerful as breakthrough improvements. Even better, incremental improvements are within the reach of every employee.

Organizations prosper when everyone is creatively engaged in seeking improvement. The benefits of a well-run quality process come in revenue generated, anticipated cost reductions and measurable increases in customer satisfaction. The most compelling reason for saying thank you may be the link between incremental improvements, saying thank you, and the bottom line.

It's Just Good Business

A program for saying thank you and for celebrating successes is the mortar that holds together the building blocks of morale and commitment, training and performance. For reasons of both style and substance, any change process must involve recognition, gratitude and celebration. By focusing on incremental improvement, by providing intermediate goals, by adding an element of humanness and fun, and by strengthening the link between top management and the other 90-percent-plus of the payroll, saying thank you brings the abstract concept of quality to life. Saying thank you bridges the gap between the rational and emotional aspects of work relationships.

Precisely because saying thank you does evoke emotion, however, the whole idea often has been viewed by "hard-headed" business people as a secondary issue. It is not. Finding ways to celebrate together and to convey recognition and gratitude by acknowledging the dignity and individuality of every employee go a long way toward ensuring a company's long-term financial health. Anyone interested in the organization's continued existence must make saying thank you a priority—and the responsibility to say thank you increases as the individual's rank in the organization increases. In short, saying thank you is good business. And all it takes is a little forethought.

III.

A Philosophical
Caution or Two

S AYING THANK YOU requires planning. It can be done
badly. You can lose ground in a number of ways: by
limiting efforts to one approach; by being insincere
or (just as damaging) by being perceived as being insincere; by having someone receive recognition at someone
else's expense; by giving only generalized recognition,
rather than pointing to specific actions; by saying thank
you too soon (and thus putting undue pressure on a person or a team) or too late (leaving people to wonder why
you slept through the original accomplishment). All of
these situations can be avoided, however. While no two
programs to say thank you will be identical in their details,
all well-implemented efforts share two characteristics:
They say thank you in a variety of ways, and they have
a personal touch.

Did Anyone Hear You Say Thank You?

Corporate programs for saying thank you are designed to
solve a perplexing problem for many leaders: determining

how to say thank you. Too often, an organization gives everyone something that either the president of the company or the head of human resources likes—under the assumption that if one of those two likes it, everyone will (or should) like it. This approach also contains an element of "fairness," which executives who are comfortable with rational scenarios find particularly appealing.

Unfortunately, not everyone "hears" thank you the same way. An expression of gratitude that thrills or at least

Figure 4.   Thank you flowchart

satisfies one person may well make someone else vaguely uncomfortable and put a third person to sleep. Take, for example, those ubiquitous engraved plaques presented to worthy employees (often in small, informal ceremonies). Although there is nothing inherently wrong with a plaque, its reception may be paradoxical. For example, Employee A may spend the evening following the presentation polishing the plaque preparatory to hanging it above the fireplace, while Employee B takes the plaque home and puts it directly into the fireplace (or if morale in the organization is sufficiently high, settles for putting it in the back of a closet with a rueful shake of the head).

As long as an organization stays within the restriction of hiring human beings, this paradox is going to exist. Author/consultant Janis Allen uses the phrase, "I sent you a circle but you received a square," to encapsulate the phenomenon.[3] What counts is what is heard and, as with every form of communication, different people "hear" thank you in different ways.

It Doesn't Always Sound the Same

A highly individualized response to an attempt to say thank you complicates matters, but neither is it an insurmountable hurdle nor should it come as a surprise. Once again, Abraham Maslow helps illuminate the reasons why different people have different reactions to the same thing: They are at different stages of personal development and have different needs. As a result, reactions to a particular gesture will vary not only from person to person, but over time, the same person will have different reactions to the same gesture as the individual's circumstances change. Even assumptions about "like" groups of people are risky. Two mid-level managers may look comparable on paper, but one may drive an old car and live in a paid-for house, while the other relishes a flashy car and has large house payments. Their records in the workplace may be identical, but their ideas of what constitutes a thank you are likely to be quite different.

Then, too, particularly in a country like the United States where cultural diversity is the norm, different cultures respond in different ways to different forms of recognition and gratitude. It is an organization's responsibility to find a way to thank everyone in a variety of ways; it is not the individuals' responsibility to be pleased with half-measures.

Effective Programs Require Options

Organizations that give only one type of recognition—be it a plaque, cash, or anything else—may have devised a fair system but not necessarily an *effective* one. There's a distinct possibility that only one person in three or four will really feel thanked and be motivated to do more. The majority may feel cheated or, perhaps worse, feel nothing.

The solution? Build a program that says thank you in several different ways to each person, leaving it to the individual to decide which particular thank you is meaningful to him or her. The saying that "The customer perceives service in his or her own terms" can be modified honestly to say, "The employee perceives gratitude in his or her own terms." What is heard in the way of gratitude for a job well done is more important than what is said. In short, if they didn't hear it, you—effectively—didn't say it. In the workplace, for both short- and long-term purposes, you don't really care exactly what rings a person's chimes—you do care that everyone's chimes get rung. Regularly. Or more correctly, whenever they deserve it.

Taking Thank Yous Personally

Something else holds true for every corporate program for saying thank you: Personal involvement is a must. As with any effort to strengthen an organization's ties with its employees, just saying it does not make it so. In 1992, Lakewood Research published a poll in which executives and employees were asked if they agreed or disagreed with the following statement: "This company genuinely cares about the well-being and morale of the employees and takes actions to help people feel good about working here." Sixty-seven percent of the executives agreed with the statement; eighteen percent of their employees agreed.[4] Lots of circles were being sent; lots of squares were being received. Disconnects traced to faulty communications occur because it is not just what the managers do, it is how they do it and their apparent frame of mind while they do it. Consider the following example concerning the use of measurement:

Imagine that Manager A were to tell Employee B to take a particular measurement every hour and to send the results to Manager A on a weekly basis. After receiving weekly reports for a month, Manager A then descends upon Employee B and announces, "A-ha! Now I know where the problems are! You're making mistakes! You better fix this right away or you're going to be in a heap of trouble." How much cooperation should Manager A expect? How quickly will the problem get fixed and how permanent a solution could be expected?

Now consider the same scenario. Again a month has passed and Manager A, four weeks of reports in hand, arrives on the scene and says, "When you have time, we need to talk. There is a problem, and since you are the one right here on the scene, I'm willing to bet that you're going to have the best ideas on how to fix things. When can we get together to start working on this?" The people are the same, the data is the same, the locations are the same, and Manager A's intent is the same. Yet this time Manager A is going to get a lot more cooperation, and the chances of a long-term solution are infinitely higher. The difference? Attitude.

Having the Right Attitude

Attitude is determined in large part by the emotional status, needs and background of the managers who are saying thank you. Some senior managers begin a program of saying thank you less-than-convinced that it is the best investment of their time. For stated rational reasons (or for emotional reasons that they may not have articulated even to themselves), they resist being involved with their subordinates in this way—even while paying lip service to the notion that employees deserve the company's gratitude. Not all such behavior is a rear-guard action to keep relationships strictly rational. Some of it results

from feelings of self-consciousness or fear of being perceived as insincere.

Sincerity Means the World

The sincerity issue crops up every time you (or anyone
else for that matter) change habits. If you have not been
in the habit of saying thank you, your initial efforts may
be met with reserve. Saying thank you requires a degree
of self-confidence. How you feel about the effort colors
the exchange. *You have to be genuinely glad that someone else
has achieved something.* Even if you are trying to establish a
bottom-line benefit, this doesn't mean that the recognition
being offered is an act of hypocrisy—any more than saying
thank you to your teenager for cleaning up a room is
hypocritical—as long as you keep the achievement in
mind. True, by saying thank you, you no doubt increase
the odds of more pleasant surprises in the future, but
that does not make the spoken words insincere. The
rational and emotional components are parallel but not
interdependent.

Practice Makes Perfect

It may seem incongruous, but anyone can be trained
to say thank you. Admittedly, the training sounds to the
casual observer like forcing someone to do what someone
else has decided is a good idea, but given a minimal
amount of cooperation and good will, behavior can pre-
cede deep emotional commitment. In short, if discussion
and study don't convince a manager (at any level) that

saying thank you is the appropriate thing to do, it is quite reasonable for senior executives to direct the manager to do it anyway—as long as the organization provides a way to say thank you. The senior person may be quite specific about actions required (for example, making it mandatory to deliver a specific number of gift certificates in a prescribed period of time). It is also desirable for the senior executive to keep an eye on the results and to offer encouragement and reminders—as often as needed—to ensure that the manager practices the designated behavior. A company doesn't simply get what it measures; it gets what it reinforces.

When people are being thanked during someone's "training period," they won't necessarily be able to tell that they are being thanked by a "trainee" as long as the trainee makes even a modest effort. People respond to behavior, not to what is carefully hidden in the (perhaps) dark recesses of an executive's heart. In an environment in which morale is already high, it's all right for an executive to be clumsy about saying thank you, particularly at first. Employees will apply the same rules to a leader's behavior that they feel are being applied to their own efforts: As long as a person is falling forward, demonstrating an effort to do the right thing and improve, a sincere effort is acceptable. It's a solid bet that after extending a small number of such not-quite-voluntary-on-his-or-her-part thank yous, the manager will relax and enjoy it.

The First Thank You Is the Hardest

In organizations in which low morale and criticism are the norm, the initial effort to make saying thank you a habit is more problematic. Any gesture, no matter how heartfelt and polished, may be met with initial skepticism or downright hostility. It helps to have some of that self-confidence. It also helps if thank yous are not separate from the rest of what is going on in the organization. Efforts to say thank you must be in step with both the published and practiced values of the company. When a disparity exists, a change in behavior on the part of executives can introduce as many problems as it solves. The only remedy is time and consistency.

Looking for a Model

To create coherence between what employees at all levels see and experience requires a realistic framework for saying thank you. To promise to be grateful for responsive external customer service and then make delivering that service difficult by imposing senseless rules (e.g., time limits on interaction) or to insist on meeting certain standards to gain recognition (e.g., for quality) without providing the tools and training to meet those standards is foolish at best, destructive at worst.

So what kind of framework is necessary? Although thank you is not particularly complicated, its straightforwardness can be deceptive. Just because this concept is based on stuff you learned as a child, it doesn't follow that it can be done quickly or at the last moment. In fact, one of the major stumbling blocks on the way to a complete program incorporating company-wide awards, team awards, and individual awards, is that the executive assigned the task of design tends to put the requirement into either the "too easy" pile or the "too hard" pile. In the former case, the executive decides that this is a minor project that can be pulled together whenever he or she has an hour or two to spare. In the latter case, the executive avoids doing anything in the hope that the requirement will go away. In both cases the executive is in for a surprise. This phase is neither too easy nor too hard. It just takes time and a hint or two to get started.

IV.

THANK YOUS BY DESIGN

<hr>

THERE ARE PROVEN PRINCIPLES that can be adopted and successful practices that can be adapted when planning how and when to say thank you. This chapter concentrates on proven principles; the next three chapters, on successful practices. It may relieve the pressure to recognize that no program will be perfect at the outset. It won't be perfect a year later, either, but it will be better. What is important is that the organization is perceived throughout the company as giving it its best shot.

In an excellent article in *Quality Progress* magazine,[5] Gene Milas identifies key attitudes and behaviors needed in establishing recognition systems as well as some guidelines for those systems:

Key attitudes and behaviors:

- sincerity

- fairness

- appropriateness

- consistency

- timeliness
- importance

Guidelines:

- Recognition is not compensation.
- There cannot be winners and losers.
- Not all successes are based on quantitative measurements.
- Recognition is not manipulation.
- Recognition is not based on luck or fate.
- Employees must contribute to the recognition strategy.
- Recognition is a personal experience.
- Recognition is fun.

Milas's guidelines are not always as self-evident as they first appear. His bias is to let employees design and run a recognition program with management as an interested bystander; he also has a strong preference for awarding individuals over groups. When he speaks of recognition as a personal experience, for example, he links achievements to *individual* efforts and cautions specifically against senior management presenting awards to subordinates, an event he feels implies some sort of "caste system." Playing lord or lady bountiful should certainly be avoided. The advantages of involving senior managers in saying thank you were spelled out in Chapter 2. Also, some people crave individual acclaim, while others feel much safer being recognized in groups. Some corporate cultures are built on teamwork without calling out relative merit. A mixture of approaches that allow for flexibility may well be more effective.

The guidelines as given above lend themselves to discussion of what constitutes a firm foundation for a thank you program. The following commentary expands on–and occasionally differs from–the explanatory notes in Milas's article.

Recognition Is Not Compensation

Money in some form will likely be a part of a recognition program–but it pays to handle that part of the program carefully. If you hand out too much cash, it may be treated as a regular part of compensation and lose its impact. At that point, people expect similar sums to be handed out regularly–deserved or not. Gift certificates worth a modest amount solve most of these difficulties. There is little danger of confusing them with incentives or fair payment for services rendered. It is, of course, impossible to completely separate the notions of saying thank you and offering financial rewards. The people who are most often thanked are almost invariably those whose energy and imagination also earn promotions, bonuses and so on at an accelerated pace. Gift certificates, however, reinforce the fact that these sums are part of a recognition program and are meant as a gesture of gratitude.

There Cannot Be Winners and Losers

To be truly effective, the organization's program of saying thank you must be available to all employees at all levels—which implies that there is a way for every employee to become involved in corporate efforts to improve. Of course, senior management can always decide to exclude some positions and people from those efforts (and thus the recognition program), but it is only fair to tell those excluded exactly why their jobs have been defined as thankless tasks. The mental image of the president of an organization approaching someone and saying something like, "Well, we don't think you will ever have an idea worth following up," is a powerful argument for 100-percent participation. It is equally important that nobody wins at someone else's expense. Although there can (and will) be competition against a defined standard, one person's gain should never be at someone else's loss.

"Available to all employees" also means that the program is designed to thank middle managers. In the United States in recent decades, too many improvement efforts tried to make a connection between senior managers and nonmanagers and skipped right over the all-important people in between on the corporate ladder. Thank you is for humans, not for any one specific class of humans. Besides, how can senior managers expect middle managers to say thank you to others if they don't hear it themselves?

Not All Successes Are Based on Quantitative Measurements

The third guideline refers to the use of quantitative measures. Of course, quantitative measurement comes into play when designing a basic scheme—but it is the spirit and not the letter of the law that you are dealing with here. Leave room for the immeasurable, such as courtesy, enthusiasm, congeniality and effort. Above all, always err on the generous side. It is far better to spend an extra fifty dollars saying thank you to someone who doesn't truly deserve it (the individual's peers will most likely make him or her "pay") than to miss thanking someone who truly deserves it.

Recognition Is Not Manipulation

Tony Rinaldo addresses the issue of manipulation in a *Harvard Business Review* article, "Rethinking Rewards," noting that "The objective of a reward plan is not 'to control or manipulate' . . . it is to provide focus and reward improved performance."[6] There is less likely to be a whiff of manipulation if a program of recognition, gratitude and celebration is linked to stated and practiced organizational values. Helping to inculcate the workforce with the desired beliefs and habits and encouraging desired behavior is not unethical, as long as those beliefs and habits are reinforced by what occurs in the organization. Milas states that recognition has to be valid, genuine and meaningful for the recipient and the giver.

Recognition Is Not Based on Luck or Fate

It may seem redundant to state that the best thank you programs are not based on luck or fate. One of the major purposes of designing a program of recognition, gratitude and celebration is to enable executives to know when it is appropriate to extend praise. If executives have the code, so should everyone else. Congratulations linked to achievement are meaningful; congratulations out of the blue are not.

Employees Must Contribute to the Recognition Strategy

How congratulations are to be extended should also be a matter of common knowledge. Any program worth the investment of time and money sets up a consistent, easily understood, "beatable" system where people know how to succeed. Employees can play a role in defining such a program. Milas recommends that a cross-level, cross-division committee of employees conducts a survey and makes recommendations to the appropriate senior management decision maker(s).[7] He feels that for a number of reasons it is good practice to form an employee committee to review recognition criteria and policies:

- It avoids anti-company or anti-management cynicism that might occur in other approaches.

- It solidifies employee cooperation, since the bestowal of recognition rests with peers rather than managers.

Thus potential roadblocks are avoided in the superior-to-subordinate relationship.

• It promotes quality and productivity efforts aimed at the internal customer (other employees).

Even this approach is not foolproof. Asking people to make rational forecasts about their emotional response at some point in the future may be accurate on a general basis but is likely to be a little shaky on an individual basis. Another potential problem may occur if the intent of the survey is not explained fully at the outset. If employees think they are turning in a "wish list" in return for "being good," a list it is the company's duty to fulfill (much like children giving their Santa list to their parents), morale problems may occur.

Employees Know Themselves

Taken on balance, however, employees do have a better idea of what they can achieve and what will make them feel thanked—often to the surprise of management. Barbara Glanz, a consultant, conducted a survey for a state government agency in the Midwest and discovered that the number-one request by nonmanagement employees was to spend a half-day in the state commissioner's office—just watching what was going on.[8] And management is free (and wise) to add frills and flourishes to a basic program as time goes on. Variety keeps programs active and vigorous. Over time, an organization will need to vary every aspect of the program—but never the intent.

Gratitude Should Be Timely

It is always a good idea to make gestures of gratitude as timely as possible. Take note of accomplishments immediately afterward whenever possible. This means that leaders need to keep in touch with what is going on while keeping enough distance not to micromanage. Leaders—much like effective parents or coaches—don't just sit on the sidelines, quietly observing before saying something. They stay involved, aware of what is going on, and offer reinforcement when needed. An annual event to say thank you has a place, but in the absence of numerous interactions throughout the year, an annual event will have minimal impact, no matter how much ceremony is attached to it.

Thanks As a Part of Corporate Culture

If the company can make the simple act of saying thank you a natural component of the company culture, continual improvement will follow. But this won't happen accidentally: The example must be set by the company in its policies and habits, and it must be demonstrated by the actions of senior managers. Remember that employees mirror the treatment they receive. If employees are treated with disdain, they will treat customers as an imposition on their time. If employees are treated like automatons, they will not extend the customer-winning behavior needed for success in an increasingly competitive marketplace.

Recognition Is a Personal Experience

Milas makes a point when he writes that individual recognition is powerful,[9] but so is the personal touch—especially the personal touch of senior management. Hearing thank you from fellow employees may be satisfying from an egalitarian point of view, but employees who make a special effort deserve to have it noticed in the executive suite. Why not arrange for both?

In any event, a personal touch is essential. There is a huge difference between sending employees "recognition stuff" through the company mail and presenting it to them in a personal way filled with warmth and gratitude. The same practical results are achieved in both cases: The employee gets the "stuff" in hand. Each case, however, results in a far different impact on the employee's feelings about the event and the company.

A Personal Touch Can Make or Break the Day

In a truly rational workplace, a committee might be able to decide on gifts of various sorts and deliver them to appropriate people in a private ceremony conducted by the mail clerk. People will even have a degree of emotional reaction to receiving such "recognition" or "gratitude." But don't bet on it being the reaction you want. For example, at a small liberal arts college in Massachusetts, the annual twenty-dollar Christmas "gift" for staff arrived in an everyday, interdepartmental envelope with a business card from the president of the college—despite the fact that the college

Figure 5.   A personal touch can make the day

was run by Jesuit priests and there was a printing department in the building fully capable of whipping up something for the occasion. Holiday feelings did not come to the fore. The department secretaries did, however, use their Christmas money for an occasion: In January they went to dinner as a group—and toasted the ineptitude of the gesture. Personal involvement on the part of someone could have salvaged the situation.

Recognition Is Fun

Finally, use your sense of humor. Don't be afraid to be silly. Make time to celebrate together. Thank you is fun!

The next three chapters include case studies featuring
long-term programs, short-term programs, and annual
bashes—a smorgasbord of ideas—and it isn't hard to
spot the element of fun in each. Setting up an effective
program of recognition, gratitude and celebration requires
time, thought and emotional commitment and expense,
but once things are sorted out, defined and operating, the
fun begins.

V.

THE THANK YOUS ARE COMING!
THE THANK YOUS ARE COMING!

WHEN PAUL REVERE INSURANCE GROUP in Worcester, Massachusetts, decided to say thank you as part of their overall "Quality Has Value" effort, they pulled out all the stops. Aware that the only safe option was to say thank you several ways, they designed a baseline program that affected everyone in the organization on a day-to-day basis and supplemented it with short-term programs—also available to every employee—and topped off both with yearly celebrations. Their long-term approach is described in this chapter; the rest of the program, in the next.

Paul Revere's goal was to establish a simple, straightforward, universal formula to signal executives when, why and how to say thank you. The key words were flexibility and common sense. The program succeeded so well that when Froedtert Memorial Lutheran Hospital in Milwaukee, Wisconsin, began its quality process, it adopted the model with only minor alterations.

The long-term program recognized teams of people. Each of the 1250 employees at Paul Revere's home office was assigned to an ongoing team made up from the natural work units. (In subsequent years, the 1250 members of the field force were also divided into teams and some teams were cross-functional.) Teams named themselves (e.g., the Dinner Belles in the cafeteria; the Marketeers in the marketing department).

One member from each team (not necessarily the most senior) received team leader training, and the company allowed time for weekly team meetings, during which teams looked for opportunities for improvement. An easily understood, progressive formula for levels of accomplishment was devised, based on Bronze, Silver, and Gold levels (see Figure 6).

Recognition was linked to achievement in a way that was wonderfully, faithfully predictable. Each person knew that, despite any individual personality faults or perceived grudges held by anyone else, if his or her team did A, all the team members would receive B. In the first year, only one team failed to make Bronze; in subsequent years, none failed.

The either/or ideas/savings formula for each level of recognition gave each team an equal chance to succeed. Some departments (e.g., Human Resources) were far more likely to make a series of small improvements— with a significant impact on customers or morale—than to implement a big budget idea. Other departments (e.g., Computer Resources) were more likely to implement grand improvements—often invisible to the customer—with a significant impact on the bottom line. Analysts checked

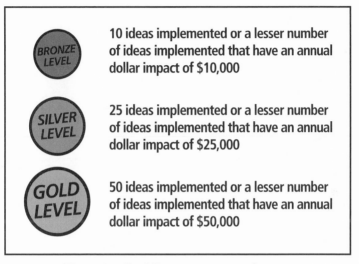

10 ideas implemented or a lesser number of ideas implemented that have an annual dollar impact of $10,000

25 ideas implemented or a lesser number of ideas implemented that have an annual dollar impact of $25,000

50 ideas implemented or a lesser number of ideas implemented that have an annual dollar impact of $50,000

Figure 6.   Paul Revere team award system

the number of ideas and savings calculations for good-faith mistakes and consistency of calculations.

Ceremonies, Ceremonies, Ceremonies . . .

What happened when a team achieved one of the levels? The person in charge of the mechanics of the recognition program (and, yes, such a person is needed for the program to succeed) called the team leader to pick a mutually convenient time for a small recognition ceremony with one of the senior executives of the company. Executives pledged to give one or two hours per week to say thank you. During the first two years of the Quality Has Value process, the president of the company and the two senior

vice presidents took part in 725 team recognition ceremonies. This huge investment in time was repaid by ideas
that brought approximately $15 million to the bottom line.
Market share also grew significantly, and employee morale
rose steadily.

The Program in Action

It's worth describing a typical, fifteen-minute ceremony to see how the philosophy and principles in the pre-
vious chapters came into play. At the appointed time, the
executive showed up in the team's work area. A common
opening remark was, "I understand you folks have made
it to the Bronze/Silver/Gold level. What did you do?" One
or more of the teammates usually leapt at the chance to
brag about what the team had done—often pointing out
one or the other of their teammates for particular praise.
Alternatively, teammates nudged someone to the front
with a statement like, "Well, Chris really had the big idea
for us this time. Chris, why don't you explain it?"

Benefits of This Approach

There were at least three benefits of this exchange:
First, the knowledge that the executive cared enough to
come to their work area and listen and learn about what
their team did was all it took to convince some people that
they were on the right track—and to motivate them to look
for even more ways to improve things. Second, individual
team members had a chance to shine, and for many of
them, the opportunity to tell the senior executive face-to-
face about what happened was all the thanks they needed.

Third, the executive also learned more about his or her company and how things actually got done.

The Material Component

Some people were profoundly indifferent to this exchange. The reaction of these team members was a silent, "Yeah, yeah, let's cut the chit-chat and get to the goodies." Since Paul Revere planned on saying thank you in several ways, "goodies" were next. During the first year, employees chose an item from one of three different catalogs, according to their level of recognition; in the second and subsequent years, when a team reached the Bronze level, each team member received one ten-dollar gift certificate; at Silver, they received two; and at Gold, they received four. Catalogs and gift certificates both reap more benefits for a company than does cash, but gift certificates were preferred over catalog items because recipients had greater flexibility in choosing an item.

A caution on cash.   From a company's viewpoint, gift certificates operate as "money with a memory," a particularly important distinction when small sums are involved. If you hand someone twenty dollars in cash as a gesture of gratitude (remember, you are saying thank you, not paying fair value for a task accomplished), the emotional buzz lasts anywhere from twelve to fifteen seconds. Then the cash goes into a purse or pocket and, effectively, disappears—to be spent on gas or groceries or whatever. (If you must give cash, give it in two-dollar bills; the U.S. Treasury printed a bunch more in 1996.)

Gift certificates are golden. A gift certificate, however, carries a built-in reminder—whether the certificate is an American Express Gift Check or a company invention backed through arrangements with a selection of stores and restaurants. (Remember that gift certificates may also be purchased for sporting events, musical concerts, cultural events, gasoline, phone calls, groceries, restaurants, and movies.) Gift certificates are taken home and shown to other family members, who most likely respond with something like, "Gosh, where'd you get that?" The answer: "Well, I work with a great bunch of folks, and we did some neat stuff and the company said thank you. In fact, the president of the company handed this to me this afternoon."

A gift certificate gives the recipient the option to purchase whatever fits his or her needs at the time. Interestingly enough, however, people don't tend to figure gift certificates into the family budget. When certificates accumulate, they are used to buy luxury goods or services, something not necessarily bought with "real money." And when the certificate(s) are presented for redemption, the store clerk may comment on how lucky the individual is to have received such a gift, which in turn is likely to elicit a favorable report on the company.

Having a store clerk or a family member hear praise for a company is a peripheral benefit; the real benefit is in having employees remind themselves how lucky they are to be working for such an outstanding company. Anything purchased with gift certificates ups the odds that the employees will remember where the money came from.

When employees look at the objects they've "purchased" with their gift certificates, a remembrance of achievement and a kindhearted feeling toward the company will arise, perhaps not every time, but frequently enough to count.

Money isn't everything. For some people, the financial token will be the thank you that they hear; for them, the reaction can be summed up as, "If you give me money, I understand you are grateful." But there are people whose reaction is, "Of course you should give me money–I'm underpaid. Now, how are you going to say thank you?" It's time to try again.

Try something symbolic. For some people, a little something that hangs on a wall, sits on a desk or is worn on a garment counts as a thank you. Some people enjoy the constant reminder that such objects provide. Also, they know that whenever someone else sees their lapel pin or charm or plaque, that person will know that the owner of the object has done good work and the company has taken the time to notice it. Others may take the item politely and deposit it in their bottom drawer with all the other pins and plaques they've received. Paul Revere used lapel pins and charms that could be worn on a chain.

Put it in print. To add to the gifts, the senior executive reminded people to watch for their names in the next edition of the company publication. For some people, public recognition of this kind carries the day. A write-up in the company newspaper can, indeed, meet any of a number of Maslow's Hierarchy of Needs. An employee new to a particular position, or to the company for that matter, can be made to feel far more secure. "They won't fire me," the conscious or subconscious reasoning goes, "not while they're saying such good things about me." Publicity enables peers to find out about the accomplishments of others and gives them a chance to say, "Good job!" As public affirmation of one's worth (also known colloquially as a "public stroke"), seeing your name in print cannot help but legitimize and strengthen feelings of self-esteem. In short, it is nice to be told that you are doing something right and that the company appreciates it in such a public way.

The final gesture. To close the ceremony at Paul Revere, the senior executive shook hands with each member of the team and offered a personal thank you. For many people, that gesture resounded the most. Oh, they spent the money, they wore the lapel pin, they took the publication home to read through and show off, but what really rang their chimes, what made them feel good all the way from the soles of their feet to the tops of their heads was having the senior executive shake their hand and say, "Thank you. I very much appreciate your effort."

Paul Revere's program was complete but not perfect. Over time, it underwent revision to a form of self-assessment with greater leeway for long-term projects. It was, however, an excellent basic program that other companies have adapted with success. McCormack & Dodge, a computer software and software services organization in Natick, Massachusetts, borrowed the formula for recognition and found that the basic numbers had to be adjusted in the second year. Silver became "15 ideas or $40,000," and the company added a Diamond level to handle the $500,000 idea that one team implemented.

Keeping the System Honest

During the first year of the Bronze/Silver/Gold program at Paul Revere, the director of quality encountered an interesting problem: People cheated, usually in one of two ways. First, the formula for recognition was so easy to use that when a team didn't have quite enough "on the books" to reach the next level before the end of the year, they waited until January 1, when all the indicators were set back to zero, before reporting an improvement. This gave them a jump-start on the next year. Second, not every member of a team performed equally well—or at all.

In the face of these infractions, the director of quality made an important decision: Keep the big picture in mind. The company was aiming for a generous, fair, beatable program that promoted the quality objectives. What counted was that every deserving person heard thank you. If it was necessary to thank a few extra people or to say thank you a few extra times to make sure that no deserving person was missed, so be it.

In the first case, manipulating the timing on reporting improvements actually acted as an incentive to look for more improvements the following year. Since the goal was continuous improvement, no harm, no foul. In the second case, these were team awards by definition. The executive making the presentation and the company were seen as being fair; the one who was perceived as unfair was the nonperforming team member. Peers usually took care of the situation with after-ceremony comments such as, "We noticed you accepted the goodies. Does this mean that it's your turn to come up with some ideas?" When peer pressure failed, immediate managers and supervisors were in a position to take care of the rascals.

Surprises, Surprises, Surprises . . .

Also, people often had unexpected reactions to being thanked. The director of quality heard from two employees who completely misjudged their own anticipated responses. The first individual, a senior executive, had chosen a clock radio from a catalog but wasn't very excited about it. After all, he had helped to define the recognition system and knew the system was built so that people who "needed" material things would get them. He just didn't need anything.

The clock radio was delivered by UPS to his home. As he was unwrapping it, one of his children came up and asked what was in the box and why it had come. As he began to explain that he worked with a great bunch of people and a company that said thank you for their efforts, he felt chills racing up and down his spine—to his own amazement.

A few days later, a nonmanagement employee told the director about his personal reaction at his team's first awards ceremony. He had previously made no bones about the fact that, while perfectly happy to take part in the improvement efforts, he extended himself because he wanted something from each catalog. At the ceremony, he was delighted to learn that each team member would be picking something from the appropriate catalog that day.

He expected nothing more. When the vice president for human resources shook his hand, looked him in the eye and said "Thank you," to his complete surprise, he felt deeply touched.

By building a program that said thank you several ways, Paul Revere was able to communicate its gratitude to every employee throughout the year. It was a wonderful basic scheme; it just needed a little something extra.

VI.

Yankee Ingenuity at Work

I T DIDN'T TAKE PAUL REVERE long to learn that the very assets of their long-term formula could also be its weaknesses. Straightforward and simple have a way of becoming dull and boring unless a little spice is added to the recipe. Supplemental long-term programs, short-term programs and annual events season a thank you program with a dash of spontaneity—as long as they are planned carefully.

Quality Coins

Take, for instance, "Quality Coins" (see Figure 7). At both the Paul Revere Insurance Group and Froedtert Memorial Lutheran Hospital, top executives were given Quality Coins to distribute. At Paul Revere, the bronze-colored coins were slightly bigger than a silver dollar and had the Quality Has Value logo on one side and the words "GOOD FOR ONE MEAL IN THE PAUL REVERE CAFETERIA" surrounded by a circle of the words "IN RECOGNITION OF A JOB WELL DONE" on the other. (A warning is appropriate here: No company should adopt this particular approach unless company executives are sure that the employees will consider a meal in their cafeteria a prize worth winning.) The coins were given out spontaneously whenever an executive heard of someone deserving a thank you.

That's what happened on the surface. Behind the scenes, there was a great deal of planning and follow-through to ensure that all executives used the Quality Coins. The president of Paul Revere, a marvelous leader named Aubrey K. Reid, Jr., required that each executive give out at least five coins each month. A list of who gave coins to whom was posted in the cafeteria. Any executives who failed to give out at least five coins had to explain

Figure 7. *Quality coins*

why at the senior management staff meeting. Given this nudge, the executives made sure to say thank you and soon discovered that (a) they enjoyed it and (b) employee morale was obviously on the rise. In fact, the requirement to find people to thank resulted in executives forming an informal network with the express mission of passing the word when someone did something right!

Froedtert's coins were silver-colored, engraved on one side with the legend "IN RECOGNITION OF EXHIBITING EXCELLENCE IN YOUR JOB" and on the other side with the hospital logo encircled by the words "QUALITY UNDERSCORES EVERY SINGLE TASK." That phrase is the source of the acronym QUEST, the name of Froedtert's quality process. The coins could be saved or traded in for ten dollars in cash. After the first several hundred coins were awarded during the first year of the process, Froedtert was delighted to note that barely half of the coins were "cashed in." For many of the employees, the memory of being thanked was too precious to surrender—at least until the occasion was repeated. Second and third coins tended to be cashed in more regularly.

Paul Revere's "PEET" Plan

Paul Revere also started PEET (Program for Ensuring that Everyone is Thanked), another approach to "planned spontaneity." At the beginning of each month, the top executives received PEET Sheets prepared by the director of quality. Each sheet included the names of two quality team leaders, their work locations, and some background about each. Sometime during that month, the executive would go to each of those people and talk with them—about anything. The meeting took place, of course, on the turf of the junior person.

One of the best things about something like a PEET program is that there is no agenda, no purpose for the get-together other than to make a connection between two humans. If stuck for a conversational gambit, the executive can always talk about the quality process or whatever other company-wide effort is taking place. What the junior appreciates the most (seniors take note) is that they each give the other a singular gift—time. As with the Quality Coins, if the executives are not faithful about making their PEET visits, it is easy to include a check-back system to identify lagging executives and allow them to explain their failure to their peers at a senior management staff meeting.

Short-term Programs

Paul Revere used a variety of short-term programs to complement the company's longer-term efforts. A month-long event, seemingly frivolous on the face of it, emphasized the idea of doing something so well that someone else was moved to say thank you. Any written thank you from a customer, internal or external, could—For One Month Only!—be traded in for a cactus. Why a cactus? First, it lent itself to a sticker on the green plastic pot with the terrible pun "I'm stuck on quality." Second, in February in Massachusetts, cactus plants are delightfully incongruous. Third, it is extremely difficult to kill a cactus plant. Some survived in the office, with yellowing stickers clinging to the side of the pot, for years. In a workforce of 1250, over 600 cacti were distributed.

Paul Revere also found that Sundae dinners are possible even if no one works on Sunday . . . as long as the company cafeteria has ice cream on hand. President Aubrey Reid came down and scooped ice cream in the cafeteria to say thank you on two separate occasions for no particular reason. The same idea could be used as a short-term program to encourage a particular behavior by awarding certificates for ice cream sundaes, either one per team member (if the desired behavior is team based) or in units of six or so (enabling a winner to treat a group of friends). A variation of the same basic idea would have senior executives serve ice cream sundaes in the cafeteria to celebrate a particular achievement.

Paul Revere looked for other ways to make employees feel valued. For example, new employees were invited to breakfast with President Aubrey Reid. And the cafeteria made Q-shaped cookies before the Malcolm Baldrige National Quality Award examiners paid a visit.

Annual Bashes

The company also sponsored two major annual events: "Qualifest," a fall festival to celebrate quality in October, and the "Quality Celebration" in December.

Qualifest

Paul Revere's Qualifest set aside a week during which teams were invited to construct displays in the cafeteria to educate other employees about their efforts and accomplishments. While many individuals shy away from making a presentation about their individual achievements, teams seem to welcome the opportunity to strut their stuff in public. To add zip, first, second and third place exhibits were awarded trophies one year. In addition to the trophies, the first-place team was given a gift certificate for lunch at a local restaurant; second-place team members won T-shirts with the Qualifest logo; and the third-place team was served coffee and pastries at their next team meeting by a "mystery guest"—who turned out to be the company president, complete with apron and bell to announce the snack cart. His informal, hour-long visit was the team's greatest award.

Quality Celebration

As with the award scheme throughout the year, the annual Quality Celebration was well served by having both a set of standard awards that people could count on from year to year (and thus set their individual or team sights on) and some special one-time awards. In the later category, for example, when Paul Revere set improvement in communications as its year-round goal, it sent out a ballot three months prior to the Quality Celebration. All 2500 home office and field employees received a ballot with the following question: "Who do you turn to in the company when you really need to know something? In short, who do you count on for good communications? Please list your top three."

The votes were tallied and the names of the top twenty communicators were announced at the Quality

Celebration. These individuals were each given a fancy fountain pen and a state-of-the-art telephone for their home. Better yet, within three weeks, the several hundred employees who had each received at least one vote got a hand-signed note from the company president congratulating them on being good communicators and thanking them for contributing to the company.

For the year-to-year component of the celebration, individuals and teams were nominated for awards by people inside the company. Although the winners' names were kept secret until the big moment (this is one of the few times when public surprises work—in large part because no winner needs to be embarrassed about beating out someone else), the system for determining the winners was kept as uncomplicated as possible. There were ten individual awards in two categories (individual customer service and team leader excellence), five team awards for service excellence, and each division highlighted its honor team. There were no first, second and third places; winners in each category were "tied for first."

This event was the company's chance to recognize individuals as well as teams. Although the superior performance of individuals is often reflected in pay raises, promotions and bonuses, these happen "in good time," not in a time frame that specifically links achievement with recognition. Also, some people's achievements often are not recognized at all. When John, one of the parking lot attendants, won an individual award for service excellence, he was being honored for always having a smile, keeping jumper cables handy, watching for flat tires, and warning people about expired inspection stickers.

In addition to the recognition and gratitude aspect of these ceremonies, the emphasis was on celebration. Balloons, music, slide shows and emotional speeches—all the stuff that so many of us hate to admit we like—added to the fun. The annual celebration re-charged the corporate batteries, reminded everyone that they were not alone in their efforts to improve, and introduced a new annual theme for the next year's continued growth and success.

You Can't Just Say It Once a Year

As the crowning point of a year-round program of creating an environment in which accomplishments are acknowledged, a company awards bash can tie a big bow on one year of successes and impart momentum to the next year. A word of caution about annual celebrations is in order, however: If you were to treat a family member—of any age—like dirt on a day-to-day basis and then, once a year, threw that person a party, what result would you expect? Especially if you regressed to your normal rotten behavior the next day? The same thing is true about annual company awards. In context, these occasions are great and can be the highlight of the year for all involved. Dropped into the calendar out of the blue, they lead to awkward questions: "How come they acted like we were human yesterday and went back to their old tricks today? Why did they decide to throw us a bone?"

Saying thank you once a year to a chosen few is a waste of time and money. The company president may as well say "This person (or team) is a winner! The rest of you are losers." Even if softened with a "Better luck next

year!," it can't be a very pleasant experience—and employees have a way of spotting the phoniness.

Imitation Isn't Always Flattering

There is one painful example of a company that tried to
copy Paul Revere's ultra-successful Quality Celebration
without creating the environment that had ensured its
success. Because of Paul Revere's ongoing recognition
ceremonies, the employees felt that they knew the senior
management team personally. One year, the nine top executives secretly rehearsed and videotaped a rap song with
lyrics thanking employees for their efforts. The costumes
consisted of fedoras and suits with broad lapels and loud
ties, the choreography was pretty basic, and the performance had a glitch or two. When it played on a large
screen set up on the stage, the employees went wild.
They recognized it for what it was—a wonderful, risky
act of gratitude and love—and they responded in kind.
It was talked about for weeks.

Guests from another company liked what they saw
and decided to do something similar at their upcoming
annual bash. They hurried out and got a horse to put
before their cart. They didn't change their improvement
efforts, they didn't improve their procedures for saying
thank you to employees, they just put a lot of effort into
a rap song.

It bombed big time. The employees didn't have any
real feelings for or about the executives as individuals.
They were just executives up there on the big screen. It
wasn't that the employees disliked the executives; they just

didn't know them. And watching a group of strangers do something silly (and do it poorly, no matter how enthusiastically) is embarrassing for everybody.

Daily Recognition Is Best

The best advice possible about saying thank you may be to make sure that employee performance in the workplace is recognized on a daily basis. Managers must be trained to know the importance of performance feedback, timely praise, and informal recognition. Consultant Janis Allen uses the phrase, "Value me, not just my results."[10] One way to meet Ms. Allen's criteria is through "listening down"–a concerted effort to train managers at all levels to do more than just "listen up" to their seniors and then proclaim down the hierarchical chain to their juniors. Listening to subordinates is a wonderful form of recognition that acknowledges explicitly the worth of the junior person. If limited to a choice between anything (or everything) in these last two chapters and listening to subordinates, go with the latter. It is best, however, to do both.

VII.

THANK YOUS OF ALL SIZES

O RGANIZATIONS OF ALL SIZES can find a way to say thank you. This chapter presents five case studies drawn from five widely dissimilar organizations: two are in service industries and three are manufacturing companies; the number of employees ranges from 14 to 22,000. The first case study provides dramatic proof that thank you is not a common-enough feature of business in the United States: The Internal Revenue Service audited the organization precisely because it heard about its recognition program!

Thank Yous Don't Have to Be Like Pulling Teeth

Dr. Mark Gjerde's Elk Grove, California, dental office received a reprieve from the IRS only after Gjerde was able to prove to an IRS agent that his fairly spectacular thank yous for his staff were, in fact, wise business investments with a proven return on investment.[11] As part of his argument, he noted that his employee turnover was unbelievably low. In California, registered dental assistants stay in one office an average of seven months; Dr. Gjerde's dental assistants have been with him from five to fifteen years—saving him thousands of dollars in direct training costs and in indirect productivity losses. He also indicated that this continuity was important to his patients. Four thousand of the community's ten thousand residents were patients of his practice.

An Unusual Approach to Thank You

To be fair to the IRS, Gjerde's approach to saying thank you to his staff of fourteen is unusual enough to merit attention: The whole office goes on trips at least three times a year—together—at Gjerde's expense, for the most part. These trips include summer and winter retreats, as well as a continuing education trip.

For thirteen years, the office has gone to Sun River Resort near Bend, Oregon, for a week in the summer. Gjerde pays for the accommodations: Each staff member gets a two-bedroom, two-bath condo complete with whirlpool bath and other amenities. Staff members can bring along as many others as they choose, whomever they figure they can fit in their condo. For a week, staff members and guests use the various options offered by the resort: horseback riding, golf, white-water rafting, and hiking, among others.

Since 1984, there has also been a winter trip, usually to a different place each year. Each employee is invited to bring along their spouse, and Gjerde picks up the entire tab. Making it an all-expenses-included outing reflects the fact that the office sometimes picks relatively expensive sites and not all employees have an equal amount of available cash. These week-long trips have been to places such as Hawaii, Walt Disney World, Cancun, the Caribbean (on a cruise) and Club Med. (And, yes, the IRS certifies this as a wise investment, too.)

Continuing education trips consist of taking the entire office to annual dental society meetings, wherever they happen to be in the country. These trips are typically four days in length. According to their employee manual, everyone is entitled to go "if their productivity warrants it." Gjerde has never had to tell someone they couldn't go but, from year to year, one or more employees will tell him that they won't be coming that year. The employees are brutally honest about their own eligibility.

Figure 8.   Thank yous don't have to be like pulling teeth

Customers Can Tell

Although Gjerde's practice has no specific program of day-to-day recognition, Gjerde reports that patients often comment on how often the staff says thank you to each other and on the wonderful, supportive atmosphere that pervades the office. Pictures from various trips adorn the walls of his office building, and patients often ask staff members about them. They also frequently ask Gjerde if he is hiring, and in fact, more than one former patient is on the staff.

Gjerde depends on staff members to make independent decisions—possible in large part because they have all been there long enough to understand each other's needs and habits—and he says thank you frequently whenever they do. Gjerde believes passionately in the "work hard, play hard" philosophy so often espoused but so rarely fully evidenced. Monthly staff meetings focus on ways to be more efficient, to use every minute while maintaining a patient-friendly environment. "Work smarter, not harder" is not just a snappy poster on the wall; it is a way of life. For the most part, his staff members work four ten-hour days per week (Saturday's eight-to-four-without-a-lunch-break stretch also counts as ten hours).

When it is time to play, the staff parties hardy. Every year, all staff members wear costumes to work on Halloween. This, too, has been turned into an office celebration. In early October, the entire staff descends on the same costume shop (after having lunch together—on Gjerde's tab) to pick that year's garb. Gjerde says that he genuinely enjoys watching his staff interact outside of the office, just as he enjoys getting to know their families during the summer trip. His assessment is simple: "My staff are special people."

High-Tech Thank Yous

MicroAge, a small computer reseller in Canada, feels the same about its 150 employees.[12] The company sets a marvelous example of saying thank you for the exciting growth and success due to employees' efforts. MicroAge strives to make recognition, gratitude and celebration as varied, easy and timely as possible. The company also makes its thank-you program dynamic, introducing new elements and retiring options nearly every year. What follows is a "snapshot" taken in late 1996.

Internal Awards

On the informal, personal side, MicroAge has a "Pat-on-the-Back" database. Using Lotus Notes, anyone can—at any time—enter a written thank you to another employee. The information is, of course, available to every employee at any of their three locations in the Province of Ontario.

The ACE (Associate-Client-Employee) Awards are a monthly occurrence that result from the votes of all employees. Nominations can be made in any of the three categories implied by the name. The award's intent is to single out those individuals who excel at one of the three aspects while, at the same time, benefiting the other two. A ballot with nominees' names and comments about them is prepared and sent to all associates, and everyone is asked to vote for one person in each category. Winners' names are published and distributed to all associates, clients and employees. Winners also receive prizes such as certificates for dinner at a fancy restaurant, and their names are engraved on a permanent plaque.

External Praise

Praise from outside the company is trumpeted within the company. Any letter received from a customer complimenting the actions of one or more employees is framed and then presented to the compliment-winning individual(s). The manager of the praise recipient(s) also receives a framed copy of the letter. Why the frame? To increase the odds that the letter will be displayed and not simply filed. A letter that hangs on a wall is a constant reminder that:

- doing something that motivates a customer to say thank you is valued by the company

- the company pays attention to individual efforts

- the company added to the thank you through the framing and the small ceremony involved in its presentation

In short, the company gets a lot of mileage out of the addition of relatively inexpensive frames.

Cash Incentives Have a Place

Several MicroAge programs involve cash awards, some based on monthly personal achievement, some on annual corporate performance, and some on customer satisfaction and quality achievement goals. In 1996, for instance, $5600 (Canadian) was available for each employee. One part of MicroAge's overall program for the past three years has been an annual assessment of the company by IBM (one of its major customer-partners) based on the United States Malcolm Baldrige National Quality Award. In the Baldrige scoring system, 1000 is the maximum point total and 500 is considered a very good score. Each employee received one dollar for each point that MicroAge scored on the IBM/Baldrige assessment.

Although the IBM/Baldrige assessment has been worthwhile to MicroAge, it is a time-consuming process. In 1996, MicroAge decided to set its sights on doing particularly well in 1997. (The goal was to win a "Gold" designation from IBM, up from the "Silver" it scored 1995.) For the 1996 calendar year, MicroAge passed on an IBM assessment, but to demonstrate its faith in its employees and their ability to reach Gold in 1997, it paid each employee $700—on the assumption that the company would have scored at least 700 points had they undergone the evaluation.

MicroAge also pays for knowledge, realizing that the more the employees of MicroAge use "the little gray cells," the stronger the company will be. Five hundred dollars is available to each employee each year for increasing personal knowledge either of the individual's job or of the company's customers' needs. The money is divided into five $100 pieces; some of the components are objective in nature and some are judged by an individual's manager.

Taking Thanks on the Road

The crown jewel of MicroAge's approaches to saying thank you is "The Trip." Whenever the company reaches predetermined financial goals—set at the beginning of the year—the whole company goes on vacation (in two shifts so that phones are never abandoned). In 1995 everyone in the company went to Walt Disney World. Employees were able to take a significant other as a guest.

To get the most mileage out of the travel investment—while modeling the kind of teamwork and innovative thinking that is the company's hallmark—volunteer employee teams are formed mid-year to explore alternative destinations. The teams are provided with information on budget limitations and turned loose to research vacation spots. They present their findings during a Fall Quality Forum, and the entire company votes on the final destination. In 1996, suggested sites (presented in often-hilarious skits) included Las Vegas, Nashville, Reno, Antigua, and the Bahamas—in fact, three different Bahamas packages were offered to the audience, one of which was the winner.

The thank-you program has paid off. In an industry with notoriously volatile turnover, MicroAge's turnover is significantly below industry average. Its profits and growth are also considerably above the average. Revenues for the company's three locations have doubled over the past five years, and the company has shown significant bottom-line improvement at the same time.

"Tri-dent" True Thank Yous

The senior management of Trident Precision Manufacturing of Webster, New York, believes that two statements about their business are intimately and inextricably linked: Each year, the average Trident employee receives some kind of public praise or reward nine times.[13] Since 1988, revenues have quadrupled to $19.5 million, and the average revenue per employee has increased by 73 percent.

In a business environment too often driven by catchy management trends with snappy names, Trident management's "breakthrough" decision was to emphasize their employees rather than their machinery. An integral part of that emphasis was saying thank you—and then saying it again, both formally and informally.

Informal Approaches to Thanks

The cornerstone of Trident's less-than-formal approach is the Atta-Boy/Girl program, through which any employee can say thank you to any other employee in a timely fashion by filling out and submitting a form. Within days, the person being thanked receives a certificate signed by the chief executive; the certificate includes the name of the person who filled out the form and adds the thanks of the senior management team.

Each month, names of Atta-Boy/Girl certificate recipients, along with brief descriptions of their accomplishments, appear in the *Trident Times,* a publication distributed to Trident's 167 employees and its almost 600 customers, suppliers and friends. The result, according to April Lusk, is a "sort of global recognition," as on their next trip to the plant, many who receive the publication seek out certificate recipients to add their congratulations.[14]

Formal Approaches to Thanks

More formally, anyone can nominate another employee for an Employee of the Month award based on any contribution to Trident's Excellence in Motion, the company's continual improvement effort. The senior management team votes on the winner (or winners—ties are common). The Employee of the Month is announced at the monthly meeting when the entire company shuts down for approximately twenty minutes to discuss progress and important news. The winning employee is given $100, a prestige parking place marked with a star, and a plaque; the winner's picture is posted next to all doors, there is a write-up in the *Trident Times,* and the "electronic crawl" in the break room displays the winner's name throughout the month.

At the end of each year, Employees of the Month are eligible for an Employee of the Year award, with the winner chosen by vote of the senior management team. The Employee of the Year receives $1500, a plaque, publicity in the Trident Times, and a picture on the Trident Wall of Fame located outside the company's assembly area. Pictures on the Wall of Fame are permanent. Among those enshrined are all Employees of the Month and the Year, as well as all those who complete a significant anniversary with the company. These people serve as role models for the company. The Wall of Fame also contains a plaque with the names of teams recognized at Trident's annual Christmas party, when all teams are thanked publicly.

The President's Award recognizes a top performer. In a typical year, the president presents an employee with $1500 for service "above and beyond" even Trident's heightened expectations.

Throughout the year, managers and supervisors have the option of awarding employees with tickets to sporting events, concerts, movies, and theatrical productions. Every effort is made to match the prize to the recipient's preferences and to include sufficient tickets for the entire family. How does Trident know what tickets are popular? According to Joe Miran, periodic surveys of employees include questions on the topic.[15]

Proof That It Works

Between 1988 and 1996, this maker of custom products ranging from simple brackets to machines that sort X-rays has seen its employee turnover drop from 41 percent to 5 percent. According to Nicholas Juskiw, Trident's chief executive, the company pushed decision-making down to the manufacturing floor and invested 4.7 percent of the payroll on training–enabling "workers to read blueprints, learn trigonometry, and speak English as a second language." Trident saw its defect-free production rate improve dramatically, from 97 percent to 99.994 percent. The emphasis on employee development and continuous improvement earned Trident a 1996 Malcolm Baldrige

National Quality Award in the Small Business category. Winning that award provided more positive publicity than the company could ever afford to buy.

A Bouquet of Thank Yous

American Greetings, a greeting card publisher, has 7000 full-time employees and 15,000 part-time employees, mostly in their sales and customer service branches. According to Harvey Levin, senior vice president for human resources, "Thank you is a universal emotion. Saying thank you is inherent in our business—but we also think it is very important."[16] Saying thank you is so important that, Levin estimates, at least 80 percent of American Greetings' employees are thanked formally for their efforts (in addition to having their birthday noted and celebrated) in the course of any one year. As Levin says, "Being thanked is part of the emotional pay that our people have a right to expect."

Beyond Thanks

Perhaps not surprisingly, the company uses American Greetings cards (identifiable by the rose on the back) when saying thank you to employees. For all significant service anniversaries (any anniversary divisible by five), Levin sends a card and a personal letter. And, of course, there are birthday cards from department heads. Levin includes a personal letter in his cards and is sure that most other department heads do as well.

In addition to the cards, there is a seven-foot Birthday Bear cut-out in the lobby of each company location. Each night, security guards post the names of all employees whose birthday is the following day—so that everyone can check on their way into work whether someone in their area is having a birthday.

At the department level, Employee of the Month programs throughout the company offer rewards consisting of a combination of cash, dinner with the boss, public recognition, and occasionally, a great parking place.

Ideas Are Important, Too

American Greetings's Bright Ideas program encourages employees to submit ideas that lead to process improvements and/or cost savings. For these ideas, employees receive 10 percent of the savings, as well as having their name inscribed on a plaque and receiving public recognition. This combination of thank yous acknowledges the basic truths that (a) different people hear thank you in different ways and (b) the important thing is that the thank you be heard by the deserving recipient.

As of 1996, American Greetings has a new award called the Chairman's Award, which is open to all full- and part-time employees. The award is designed to recognize extraordinary customer service, innovation, personal initiative, teamwork, and/or community service, including acts of heroism. Anyone who receives the Chairman's Award has dinner with the Chairman, receives a plaque, and is given money for self-improvement (e.g., to cover seminar or community college enrollment fees).

Recognition beyond the Workplace

The company also supports volunteerism on the part of its employees. Breakfasts are held periodically (during work hours) for all volunteers; and local leaders are invited to these breakfasts as guest speakers. At one of the breakfasts that Levin arranged, 340 employee-volunteers were recognized, and the speaker was the mayor of Cleveland. American Greetings wants its employees "to feel like their contributions are significant—which, in fact, they are."

American Greetings also works at having fun in the workplace as a way of celebrating the company's continued success. At Halloween, for instance, everyone is encouraged to decorate their office space and to come to work in costume. During the day, there are competitions for best costume and for best carved pumpkin. There is even a Halloween Tunnel, offering a ten-minute journey through darkness and fright . . . with lots of horrifying screams and dangling things to speed the journey. Employees are encouraged to bring their kids.

For the holidays, American Greetings gives each employee a holiday turkey—and then asks them if they would like to contribute to the drive to feed the hungry. Many give back their turkeys—and additional food. The company newspaper applauds the departments that do the most toward helping the food drive, and the company supplements all employee contributions. The holidays are also occasions for periodic Open Houses to thank everyone for their efforts on a general basis and to give employees a chance to have their families see where they work and enjoy some holiday refreshments at the same time.

Weaving Thank Yous into the Fabric of Your Work

With 15,000 employees, it isn't surprising that Tom Malone, the president and COO of Milliken & Company, a winner of the Malcolm Baldrige National Quality Award in 1989, has put a lot of thought into the idea of gratitude and the role it plays in the workplace.[17] He points out that America is a sports-mad country and that the number-one event is the Super Bowl. He offers the following reasons for its popularity:

- the right environment
- the right teams
- the right coaches with the right game plans (he sees senior management as the coaches)
- a scoreboard so that you can tell who is winning
- most valuable players
- fans in the stands, applauding and cheering those doing the work
- championships

Malone says that Milliken tries to create the same environment by recognizing and applauding its over 15,000 employees—"the right teams"—as much as possible. The scoreboards are kept throughout the organization, and senior management becomes the fans in the stands, applauding the teams and individuals making break-throughs. No company gets to the Super Bowl without all the ingredients on Malone's list. At Milliken, one senior manager describes the current environment as one in which they encourage "benevolent discontent about every-thing from customer treatment to landscaping."

Opening the Floodgates to Improvement

Ironically, when Milliken first asked its employees for their ideas, there was little response. Since the company has long believed in and practiced decentralization, senior managers at each location were urged to try different approaches to encouraging employees to submit ideas. One manager promised his employees that if they submit-ted an idea he would acknowledge receipt of the idea—a simple form of saying thank you—within twenty-four hours and that he would make sure that the employees knew what would be done about their ideas within seventy-two hours. The dam of ideas broke. This same practice is now practiced throughout Milliken—known simply as the "24/72 Rule"—and is the backbone of their employee idea system that now averages sixty-five ideas per employee per year. Over 85 percent of ideas submitted are implemented, often by the same people who submitted them; and over 90 percent of the employees receive a thank you each year.

There is no monetary recognition at Milliken. The company believes that employees are not motivated by money: They want to be appreciated, they want to be part of the decision-making process, and they want to be recognized. The results back up its belief: Gratitude expressed in ways other than cash can be a powerful tool in the workplace.

Sharing Rallies

A cornerstone of the Milliken culture is "sharing rallies," during which employees stand up and explain what they have done, individually or as a team, to improve the operations at Milliken. In attendance, and eager to applaud and cheer, are the senior management team and hundreds of fellow employees. To date, there have been over 120 sharing rallies throughout Milliken. At the headquarters location alone, where rallies are now held every ninety days, there have been fifty such rallies. Upon reaching number fifty, statistics were compiled and it was determined that, as part of these first fifty rallies, 10,000 letters of thanks and recognition had been sent out by senior managers—and over a mile-and-a-half of photographs taken and distributed.

Milliken keeps more serious statistics on an ongoing basis. For instance, it keeps careful track of who gets recognized in the course of a year. In 1995, 90 percent of all employees received some form of recognition at least once.

A Team Approach

Some of this recognition is for team efforts. The corporate headquarters has eighty quality improvement teams. Each year, the teams pick their "most valuable" team members, and those team members and their families attend a major celebration event—for example, dinner, entertainment, a reception—that includes senior management and the employees' immediate supervisors.

Management Doesn't Always Know Best

Leaders at Milliken say that management often can be as much a hindrance as a help. In fact, Craig Long, who leads the quality effort at Milliken, says that the "management of other people is non-value-added work." And when senior executives make mistakes saying thank you, he notes that it is somewhat humbling to "find out that the employees are smarter than we are."[18] He cites as an example one reward program. For one month, an employee was allowed to park in a specially marked "prestige parking place." One month, the winner failed to use the parking place. When she was asked why she was ignoring her prize location, she explained that the location was a quarter of a mile from the place where she actually worked. It was, however, close to where the executives who chose it worked. (Incidentally, there are no executive parking places anywhere at Milliken.) Now when someone wins the "prized parking place," the winner designates what parking place they want.

People Come First

Milliken's thank yous are effective because the company has an absolute commitment to quality. Long tells, with some exasperation, about companies who come to Milliken-conducted classes looking for quick fixes to their own problems. There are no quick solutions, he says: "First you have to get your people issues right. But if your employees don't trust you, if your processes aren't right, you can't hope to reach your potential."

Postscript: And, in Closing . . .

We recognize that it sounds simple: Say thank you and success will be yours. The principle really is that straight-forward, but putting it into play requires a significant investment of time, energy, ego and resources.

Please note when reviewing any of the case studies included in this book that saying thank you requires both an appropriate environment and a focused, consistent effort—but that's what leadership is all about.

Fortunately, saying thank you is a lot of fun. And the financial track records of organizations that say thank you well and often is very strong.

And yet . . . And yet . . . When all is said and done, it will require a leap of faith to change habits and make saying thank you an automatic response. A hop of hope will not suffice.

Rest assured, however, that no matter what business you are in, saying thank you to human beings has a positive and lasting effect. Use the ideas presented in this book to help you lead others into the twenty-first century.

Good luck. And thank you.

References

1. Bob Nelson. *1001 Ways to Reward Employees.* (New York: Workman Publishing, 1994), p. 130.

2. Tony Ronaldo, "Rethinking Rewards," *Harvard Business Review,* November–December 1993, p. 42.

3. Janis Allen with Gail Snyder. *I Saw What You Did & I Know Who You Are,* (Tucker, Georgia: Performance Management Publications, 1990), p. 63.

4. Lakewood Publications Survey. January 1992, 8.

5. Gene H. Milas. "How to Develop a Meaningful Employee Recognition Program," *Quality Progress,* May 1995, pp. 140–141.

6. Tony Ronaldo, "Rethinking Rewards," *Harvard Business Review,* November–December 1993, p. 42.

7. Gene H. Milas. "How to Develop a Meaningful Employee Recognition Program," *Quality Progress,* May 1995, p. 141.

8. Randall Johnson. "Rewards & Recognition: Do They Punish or Polish Performance?," *Total Quality Newsletter,* May 1994, p. 3.

9. Gene H. Milas. "How to Develop a Meaningful Employee Recognition Program," *Quality Progress,* May 1995, p. 141.

10. Janis Allen with Gail Snyder. *I Saw What You Did & I Know Who You Are,* (Tucker, Georgia: Performance Management Publications, 1990), p. 76.

11. Mark Gjerde, DDS. Conversation with authors, October 1996.

12. Tracey Hare Connell. Conversations with authors, September–October 1996.

13. Del Jones. "Training and service at top of winners' list," *USA Today,* October 17, 1996, 5B.

14. April Lusk. Conversation with authors, October 1996.

15. Joe Miran. Conversation with authors, October 1996.

16. Harvey Levin. Conversation with authors, October 1996.

17. Tom Malone. Conversation with authors, October 1996.

18. Craig Long. Conversation with authors, October 1996.

Further Reading

Allen, Janis with Gail Snyder. *I Saw What You Did & I Know Who You Are,* Tucker, Georgia: Performance Management Publications, 1990.

Hale, Roger L., and Rita F. Maehling. *Recognition Redefined,* Minneapolis, Minnesota: Tennant Company, 1992.

Nelson, Bob. *1001 Ways to Reward Employees,* New York, New York: Workman Publishing, 1994.

Townsend, Patrick L., and Joan E. Gebhardt. *Commit to Quality,* New York, New York: Wiley & Sons, 1986.

Townsend, Patrick L., and Joan E. Gebhardt. *Five-Star Leadership: The Art and Strategy of Creating Leaders at Every Level,* New York, New York: Wiley & Sons, 1997.

Townsend, Patrick L., and Joan E. Gebhardt. *Quality in Action: 93 Lessons in Leadership, Participation, and Measurement,* New York, New York: Wiley & Sons, 1992.

ABOUT THE AUTHORS

Patrick L. Townsend is a noted speaker and consultant on leadership and quality. From 1983 to 1987, he directed and coordinated the most active employee participation process in the country, a process for which he designed the recognition, gratitude and celebration component. In just three years, the 250 quality teams at the Paul Revere Insurance Group implemented over 20,000 ideas, saving the company $16 million.

Together with Joan E. Gebhardt, he co-authored the best-selling book *Commit to Quality,* as well as *Quality in Action: 93 Lessons in Leadership, Participation, and Measurement* and *Five-Star Leadership: The Art and Strategy of Creating Leaders at Every Level.* Both authors can be reached at the following address:

Townsend & Gebhardt, Advisers on Leadership and Quality, 93 Winfield Road, Holden, MA 01520